THE CHAOTIC
SILENCE

YASHVI ITALIYA

BlueRose
Publishers
NewDelhi • London

First Published in January 2022

ISBN: 978-93-5472-780-1

BLUEROSE PUBLISHERS

www.bluerosepublishers.com

info@bluerosepublishers.com

+91 8882 898 898

Cover Design:

Geetika

Typographic Design:

Namrata Saini

Distributed by: BlueRose, Amazon, Flipkart,

MESSAGE FOR THE READERS

Before you proceed,

I am extremely thankful to you for joining me and my words in this beautiful yet chaotic journey. This collection of poem comes from a sad mind. It is meant to silence your chaos and create chaos in silence.

I would also like to give a trigger warning. A few poems are based on mental illnesses and suicide. And some also mention abuse.

You are good to go now and enjoy reading it as much as I enjoyed writing it.

*In silence, I live
In the chaos, I breathe*

Somehow, I did not notice
That you were making peace
So that you can have a war
With the most delicate part of me

My heart

I paint poetry on the wall

In the colour of danger; red
I paint sexual abuse
I write how I was treated
Like a Barbie doll
Used like a tissue
And thrown away like garbage

In the colour of plants; green
I write about all the people
Who treated me right
And helped me grow
Into a beautiful flower

In the colour of peace; white
I write about the chaos within
And the calm that follows after

I paint poetry on the wall
To remind myself
About the battles I have fought
About the battles I have won

I was hoping
To be your tomorrow
But you wiped me away
From the core of your past too

The difference between
You and him is
He left me for himself
And you left me for her

She talks about pain
Like it is the only thing she feels

It *is* the only thing she feels

Halfway through life
And I already feel tired
Of living
Breathing
My heart beating

Is there any highway to reach death?

Call me delusional
For I see things
That is not real
Maybe that is why
I mistook your touch
For a touch of love
When in real
It was more than abuse

He takes care of me
Even though I am not delicate
For that is the real care
The other one is just pity

Sitting on the edge
Of an astounding bridge
I see the sun settle
Settle for what it deserves

I slowly walk back in memory lane
And see myself settling
Settling for less
So, so less, I almost lost myself

I sit there
Until the moon unhide itself
From between the heavy clouds
Which were about to rain

I remember my past
How I felt so heavy from within
That I rained
On the only person I had

I slowly get up and walk back home
A home I never called mine
It was always ours to call
But he left quicker than I could decipher

I recall calling him mine
Whereas he was not even his own
So alone and lonely
He preferred death over love

My head spins
Heart hurts
Body aches
Hands tremble
Legs shake
And they say
Depression
Is just an act

I wish I could tell them
That mental health is no joke
It sweeps you off the ground
Makes you fly up above
And pushes you down hard

You hit the ground
With so much force
That every part of your body
Which was aching earlier
Breaks into pieces

You either pick them up
Or just lay there numb

12

Nothing could match
The story of you and me
We were two villains
Ruining each other

I wish my sanity could rise
From its deathbed
And slap the faces of those
Who killed it years ago

I know only I have the right
To make or break my dream
But I do not know how
It was snatched away
Right from my hands
And broken into pieces
Which are difficult to manage

Nevertheless,
I picked it up
And put them into a coffin
I put flowers
On the grave
Of my dead dream
To bestow peace

Between a stormy night
I see darkness consuming me
So I open my eyes
And see a shade darker
I feel tears rolling down my cheek
And my palms tremble

The thunder did not stop
Neither did the rain
For a moment there
I felt like I am a hurricane

We kept eating in silence
Neither of us tried to speak
For we knew
Talking about pain
Will dig the pit deeper

What we didn't know was
That being quiet
Will move us out of the pit
And directly throw us into the grave

I wish our lips could have met
Like rain meets the earth
The storm tries to stop
But thunder is adamant
No matter how much the wind tries
To stop their rendezvous
The rain falls flawlessly
Dropping on the land
Kissing each other
After a long, long time
The thunder roars
To celebrate them
And storm silently falls apart

At the end, they meet
Unlike our lips

It hurts
Because it is happening
Once again
But it isn't painful
Because it has happened
So many times before

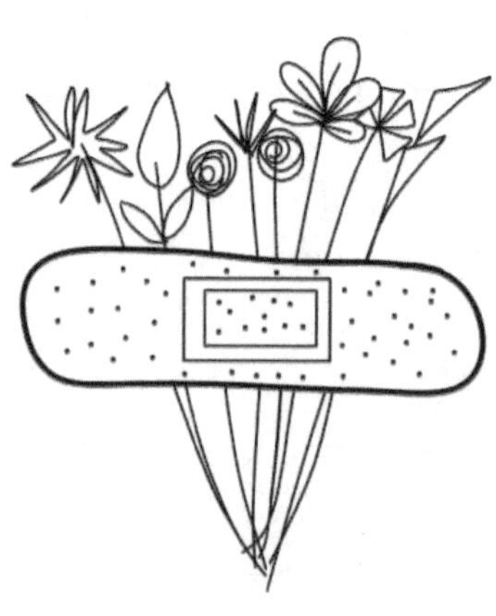

Eyes bleak
So are my emotions
But then why is my forehead
Sweating so much
And my lungs fail to breathe?
Why are my palms dancing?
And eyes rolling back?
Is it another attack?
I hope not
Because living was expensive
I switched to surviving
Now that surviving is difficult
I can't switch to death

In my dark, clouded sky
I had a few star friends
They went with me
Through light and dark
But no one stood by
When my light started fading
And glow on my face
Became nothing but pale
No one stood by me
When I needed them
For moral support

'Why did you all leave?'
I asked

'We were never really there.'
Their answer shook me

Oh, you delusional mind

After waiting for years
To fall in love
Not with others
But myself
I realised that
You don't have to fall
In love with yourself
You need to rise in love

While I kept wondering
Why you left me
While I spent my time
Forgetting you
I missed out
An important part of my life
I missed loving someone

I missed loving myself

I fell asleep
To dream
But it looks like
Nightmares
Are on duty today

Everyday

24

I couldn't fathom the truth
That a part of me is changing
When I finally accepted it
I was thrown, face first,
Into another truth
That I have changed
Not a part but all of it

The voices in my head
Want me to follow my dream
But the silence on my lips
Fail to do so

It's not so
That I deny fighting
I do
But tell me one thing
Will you fight
If your opponent
Is no one else
But you?

The cloudy weather
Only reminds me
Our cuddles
Kisses
And peace
That we always shared

When the lightning strikes
I realize that our story
Was not about romance in rain
But rather
About hurdles in hurricane

Yashvi Italiya

The sound of thunder
Doesn't scare her
She is a hurricane
Dressed in rain

When people ran away
To shelter their safety
I stood there silently
Growing between the storm
I know it is not the proudest moment
But it is definitely courageous

Do not doubt my growth
For I lived there
Where no one dared to do so

There are different stories
Told by different people
But isn't it weird
That people trust gossip by others
More than the author of the story?

You used our past
To build your future
And I used my past
To build our future
The difference
Is not a lot when spoken
But a lot when done

Nightmares are afraid of her
For she herself
Is the queen of hell

He left her is pieces
Now she picks them up
One by one
With bleeding fingers
To heal the broken parts

He left her
But she did not leave herself

Too many things on my mind
Then why do you top the list?
Our memories play in loop
I see you smile
And I fall in love once again
I see you laugh flawlessly
And I start laughing too

You see? You made me laugh
When even smiling was not possible

I don't see the good part
In every single thing
For I am not too blind
To ignore my pain
And focus on the good

I see what the reality is
If it is sad, it's sad
If it's happy, it's happy
No questions asked

I have seen a lot of
Welcome and goodbye
But what makes more sense is
I have seen people express
Express their emotions
Emotions that are deep rooted
Emotions that come out
Only at the departure
Emotions that only come out
At the thought of not seeing them

I remember
How I was left alone
To pick up my pieces
And put them back in place

I remember
How people were present
But all they did was enjoy it
As if I am performing

I remember
How I forced myself
To join my pieces
And move on in life
With cracked corners

I remember everything
As if it happened just yesterday

Oh wait, it did happen yesterday

We separated
But our memories
Are still together

They celebrate us
On our anniversary
They cry on our
Separation
They laugh at our
Lame jokes
They sleep on our bed
They cook together
They smile together

They do everything together
That we couldn't do

I see the stars break
I wonder if they see me
Shatter into pieces too

If it wasn't for life
Death would have survived

I want pain to escape
But how would it
When I am keeping it
Tight in my embrace?

I want pain to escape
But I also want it
To stay with me
So I don't feel lonely

I want pain to escape
But I keep it safe
In all of my body

They talk about my body
Like it is their own

Wait,
Would they judge
Their own body
From its very core?

Your apologies
Doesn't matter now
What you did in past
Ruined my future
And saying sorry
Cannot correct it

43

Your eyes shine
Like it holds
A hundred stars

Imagine the moon
In my eyes
Falling for the stars
In yours

One star would shoot
The moon would flicker
One star would twinkle
The moon may get shy

Imagine the romance
Between the moon and stars
And our lips celebrating
Their togetherness

This stupid heart
Keeps looking for you
In every other person
Even when it knows
That you are the last person
It should ever look for

The people who clapped
On my success
Are hiding somewhere
When I need them
The people who stood by
On my failure
Are still here
Clapping on my success

Types of people

The night gets colder
And so does our relationship
There is love
Enough love
But love is not enough

We are both striving
For a comfortable lover
In each other
And all we find is
A cold one

They say I am enough
But maybe,
Enough is not enough
For me to love myself

Travelling from one emotion
To another
My feet are tired now
For I subtly knock their door
Every time I visit
And they trespass my boundaries
With chaos and only chaos

49

You heal my wounds
The brokenness underneath
You stitch the pieces
And clean the scratches

You caress me
When I am in pain
You pamper me
When I am sad

You love me
When I don't love myself
You be with me
When I am not with myself

You do everything for me
And wonder what makes me
Love you so much

One morning
I wake you up
Only to see you
With hangover throbbing in your head
I look in your eyes
And I swear
I have never seen
Something so dark yet relieving
I can see the gloominess
But I also spot joy lurking around
I can see fear
But I also notice you're daring to explore

What is love
If not looking
In his coffee eyes
And forgetting
The world around?

What is love
If not holding
His rough hands
And walking miles?

What is love
If not being supported
And being a support?

52

I stare into the space
The space that I wish was mine
It's not like you didn't give me space
It's just that you gave too much of it

So much that I choked on air

Sunshine looked nice on you
But I couldn't preserve it for more
I saw darkness approaching you
How you fell for it completely
And then, I saw it consume you

54

The difference between
You and him is
He wanted me to wither
And you wanted me to grow

My body is a home
To imperfections
To scars
To hatred
To judgments
To expectations
To abuse
To violence

Everything except self-love

Letter by letter
I write your name on paper
I write what you promised me
I write about our love
I write about our memories
For you have left me
But the letters won't leave

57

I injured my body
Some outside
Some inside
They saw the scars
On my knee
Elbow
Fingers
Forehead

What about the scars inside?

You smell like petrichor
I love it
When the rain falls
But the moment it goes
The reality appears
And your smell
Leaves with a melancholy
A feeling that does not belong to me

It didn't matter
That I lost friends
What hurt was
I lost the meaning of
Friendship

I don't know
Who is going to visit
My grave

But I do know
Who is not

I am struggling to breathe
The air is enough I guess
But anxiety makes it difficult
It kicks in, right when it needs to leave
But who am I to stop her
When my body is a home to it

62

I was freed from pain
Yet trapped in worry
Worry of seeing pain again
In its rawest form
Worry of feeling pain
In its toughest form

New problems take birth
Every single day
I wish to break them down
And solve it bit by bit
But they come in a bunch
And hit my head hard
Wrecking my nerves
Spoiling my mood
Torturing my soul

Tell me, how do I solve them
When I don't even know the root cause?

What do I celebrate?
The days that I was
Caged in my own home?
Or the days when even freedom
Didn't help me breathe

What should I be thankful for?
The days I have spent alone
And feeling lonely inside?
Or the days when even friends
Couldn't scare away loneliness?

I am tired of being told to smile
How do I smile when I know
That just smiling is not enough
To let happiness in?

My breath hitched
When he came closer

He tickled me
On my waist

His one hand
Touched my cheek

And other went
Towards south

My breath hitched
Once again

Not out of love
But fear

The difference between making love and abusing
Lies in just one word

Consent

66

I wanted my body
To be a muse
To an artist
But it somehow became
A topic for body shaming

Some nights
I fall asleep quickly
Some nights
I stay awake

The difference is
When I sleep
I see nightmares
And when I don't
I live the nightmares

68

Sadness consumed me whole
Now I don't know
How much of me is me
And how much of me is sadness

The person in your head
And the person in real
Are two different beings
If you love one
It doesn't mean
You love the other

Dreams have a habit of breaking
Just like pain has a habit of returning
I keep dreaming
And when it breaks
Pain returns

The scorching sun
Burns my fresh scar
That is when I realize
That prince and princess
Are just two characters
Of a dreamland story

In reality,
There's no princess
There's no prince
And the kiss
The kiss is sometimes
Followed by abuse

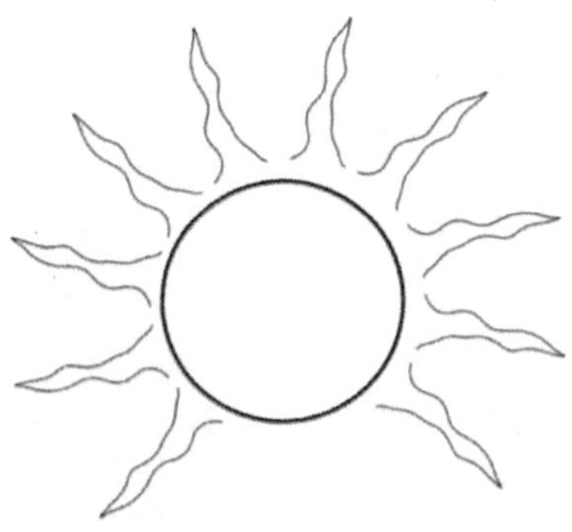

72

A lone tear
Escapes my eye
In the name of
My loneliness

73

What were you thinking
When you left me in the storm?

That I'd curl down and cry?
That I'd stand there frozen?
That I'd regret loving you?

If yes, you don't know me

I am my own knight

74

When I feel lost
In our memories
I call happiness
To sweep me away
From the ground
But all it does is
Push me harder
I bruise my body

Happiness escapes
And pain settles in my soul

In a brief moment
Eternity breathed

She has an ocean inside her
When he touches
She releases

She tastes like heaven

I met grief
On a lonely night
It met me as a saviour
I was consumed in pain
Pain of being alone
Pain of being lonely
Pain of having no one
To hug me a piece of comfort

It was strange at first
To see Grief sitting besides
Giving me a shoulder
That no one else offered
But slowly it became
My best friend

78

I am looking for love
Where despisement breathes

I am looking for love
In myself

Unwilling to separate
I know we were adamant
But time brought a series
Of unfortunate events
I know the distance is a lot
But so is our love
We may not trust the miles
But we trust our love, don't we?

Desirable pair of lips
They are soft and welcoming
When our lips touch
A volcano erupts inside

Trust me
You don't want to feel numb
Because when you do
The tears dry up
On your cheeks
And when you try to fake a smile
It stretches, making you wince
It makes you realize
That pain hasn't left
It is sitting right outside the door
Waiting for the numbness
To fade away with time

I did not lose myself
I was pulled away from myself
And thrown into fire

The phoenix rose
I burnt
And the ashes are still here
Stored in my memories

I am not able to empty it
For it is a part of me
It is me

I feel sad
When I think about my past
The worst days
The painful days
Sleepless nights
And suicidal thoughts

But I feel a sense of relief
When I realize
That it is all gone now
It will never happen again
It will leave me
And let me live

But what are the chances
Of going through worse
Than the worst?

There was a battle inside me
A battle of emotions
Where pain was winning
And happiness was all injured

I was looking for inner peace
Here and there
Everywhere
Anywhere
You know where I found it?
Under the sharp sword of chaos
You know in what state it was?
Almost dead

He left me in a mess
That I never opted to organize
There are broken pieces
Of my broken soul
Blood all around

No one would like to collect
All the pieces
And make their hands bloody
Again

Right?

Love and hate
Are two extremes
With a lot of stages
In between

It takes a lot of time
To go from hate to love
Do you know the twist?
It just takes
One moment
To go from love to hate

Why am I not surprised?

She is a chaos
Looking for a peaceful place
And it is not surprising
The she found it
In his arms

The clouds keep raining
My eyes don't stop either
There is thunder and lightning
People can see the one in the sky
But what about the one inside me?

The lightning burns my sanity
Insane, I roam around
The thunder doesn't startle me, though
I am addicted to chaos

I never thought that
The touch that soothes me
Will sting so much

I never thought that
The wild kiss
Will turn into violence

I never thought
The love of my life
Will be the reason to end life

Mixed weather
Mixed emotions
The sweat is dripping
From your forehead
But your words are nothing
But a glacier
Working hard
To melt it
Meanwhile
Losing myself
One step at a time
I am left in the cosmos
Alone
Shattered
Meaningless

Just like this poem

The high mountains
Only makes her wish
To jump from the top
It doesn't scare her a bit
It only scares others
For she thinks
She is not important
But to others
She is a queen

Come, sit with me
I want to share a tale
A tale of you and me
That turned into a tale
Of you and her

Oh, you already know that

Don't you?

If smile is contagious
Then why are so many people
Battling pain?

Some really laugh
Some just fake it
And the rest
They don't bother

If smile is contagious
Then why do I get sad vibes

Some say they are happy
Some say they are not
And the rest
They don't bother

If smile is contagious
Why are you laughing
But I am frozen?

94

What they see is
A sleeve of tattoos

What they do not know is
There are scars underneath

Scars which were too beautiful
For their judgemental eyes

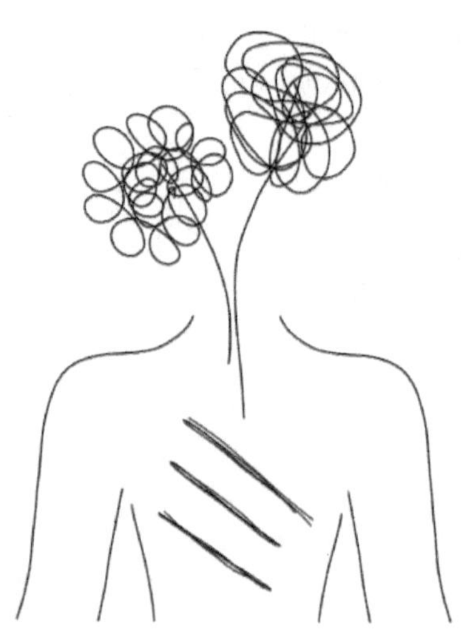

You heal parts of me
Which are not just broken
But also missing

Missing from its place
Lost in the abyss
Found almost dead

Dead since ages
No one dared to touch
And you, you embraced

I take care of triggers
When I talk about
My depression

I wish my mind could give the same

To you,

The pain you are battling, the smile you are faking, the tears you are ceasing, the breath you are choking on, I get it. I get it completely. I just want one favour from you: hold on. Hold on for a bit longer. You cannot see it from where you are, but everything is slowly falling into place. The people you lost are not replaceable, but someone better is on their way. The time you lost crying will not return, but there is happiness wandering in your future. The disconnection you felt from yourself is about to turn into self-love. The baggage of pain you are carrying on your shoulder is about to be taken off. The constant battle between joy and sadness is about to end.

I cannot tell you when the pain is going to leave because it doesn't happen overnight. It will slowly fade away from your life. Till now, you only saw the darkness lurking around the stars, but now, you will slowly notice that in darkness is where the stars shine.

We have heard about the calm before the storm. But no one talks about the calm that follows after the storm. The calm is about to reach you. Embrace you. Love you.

The calm will reach you only if you wait for it to arrive. Just hold on for a bit more.

Love,
Yashvi

THANK YOU FOR HAVING A RENDEZVOUS WITH MY WORDS

I HOPE YOU ENJOYED THIS LITTLE DATE.